WHEN LIGHTNING STRIKES

STRIKES

Questions, Beliefs,
Tales, and Tips

Della Cohen

GReaT S✳uRCe®
EDUCATION GROUP
A Division of Houghton Mifflin Company

Reading Advantage Authors
Laura Robb
James F. Baumann
Carol J. Fuhler
Joan Kindig

Project Manager
Ellen Sternhell

Editor
Jeri Cipriano

Design and Production
Preface, Inc.

Photography and Illustration
Front cover, p. 18 © Jack Novak/SuperStock; pp. 1, 8 art by Stephen
Marchesi; pp. 6, 16bl © A & J Verkaik/Corbis; pp. 10, 12, 30 © Corbis;
pp. 13, 14, 21 art by Kathie Kelleher; p. 16t © JBLI/Weatherstock; p. 16br
courtesy of NOAA Photo Library; p. 17 map art by Sue Carlson; p. 22
© Clyde H. Smith/Getty Images; p. 23 © Warren Faidley/Weatherstock;
p. 24 courtesy of Walter de Maria

Printed in the United States of America

International Standard Book Number: 0-669-51399-7

2 3 4 5 6 7 8 9 10 – RRDC – 09 08 07 06 05

CONTENTS

Introduction

Have you ever heard this joke?

Q *What does thunder have to say about lightning?*

A *It's shocking!*

This is not the funniest joke in the world, but it is true. When lightning strikes a person, it can shock, injure, and even kill the person. That's because a lightning bolt is charged with electricity.

Lightning can go in several directions: from a cloud to the ground, from the ground to a cloud, and from a cloud to a cloud. It's impossible to predict!

Lightning is powerful and dangerous. But it is also fascinating and beautiful to watch. It's nature's fireworks, and the "shows" are great. The streaks and flashes light up the sky in different ways. We just need to be in safe places to watch these shows!

Every lightning "show" is different.

Do you have questions about lightning? Are you interested in stories of surviving lightning strikes? If so, you can satisfy your curiosity about lightning by reading the following pages.

Now, on to a little bit of lightning history. Then be ready for questions and answers about lightning. Discover some beliefs about lightning. And learn about a few amazing stories of survival.

CHAPTER 1

A "Touch" of History

We owe many thanks to Benjamin Franklin for a number of things in our lives. He was a printer, a writer and publisher, a scientist, an inventor, and more. He played a big part in the development of our country and helped write the Declaration of Independence.

It is Ben Franklin, the scientist and inventor, who "connects" us to lightning and electricity. Franklin was one of the first people in the world to experiment with electricity. He did several experiments with electricity in the late 1740s.

It was in 1749 that Franklin wrote what was similar between electricity and lightning. He said that they both gave light and that the color of the light was the same. He also wrote that both traveled in a crooked direction, made a crackling noise, and were conducted by metals. In addition, electricity and lightning could hurt people and animals and set fire to certain materials.

Franklin did several kinds of experiments with electricity. His most famous electrical experiment took place in Philadelphia in 1752. He set out to prove that lightning is a form of electricity. He attached a pointed wire to the top of a kite he had made. Then he attached a key to the end of the kite string.

Franklin flew the kite into a rain cloud during a thunderstorm. When lightning struck the kite, the lightning traveled down the kite string to the key. Then Franklin touched the key, and ZAP! He received a shock. If the lightning bolt had been any stronger, Franklin might have been hurt or even killed.

Franklin proved that lightning involves electricity. Because his kite string was wet, and because water conducts electricity, the electricity from the storm was carried to the key.

In Franklin's time, buildings and other structures were often struck by lightning and burned to the ground. Franklin wanted to stop this from happening. He suspected that if he could rig up a device to attract the static electricity from a cloud and redirect it away from a building, the problem would be solved. In 1750—two years before the kite and key experiment—he invented the lightning rod. Forms of this invention are still used today. As a result, buildings are much safer.

Franklin's lightning rod was about eight feet long. It was made of iron and sharpened to a point. It was placed on top of buildings and connected to a ground rod by a wire or cable. The ground rod was buried in the ground.

Benjamin Franklin's lightning rod

About his invention, Franklin wrote ". . . the electrical fire would, I think, be drawn out of a cloud silently, before it could come near enough to strike. . ." He was right; his lightning rod redirected the electricity away from the building and into the ground. It worked exactly as he had hoped.

We have learned a lot more about lightning since Franklin's day. One thing we now know is that lightning is similar to static electricity. Have you ever rubbed the soles of your shoes on a carpet and then touched a doorknob? Whap! This may have resulted in a small spark or a minor shock. That small shock is static electricity, and it is similar to a lightning strike.

But lightning is much more powerful than a static electrical shock. In fact, the electric power from an average lightning flash could keep a one-hundred-watt bulb burning for about three months. Now that's powerful!

Read on and you'll find lots of questions and answers about lightning and electricity in the next chapter.

CHAPTER

2

Q's and A's about Lightning

How often does lightning strike?

Lightning strikes somewhere on Earth fifty to one hundred times every second! That comes to eight or nine million strikes every day.

What exactly is lightning (and thunder)?

Lightning is a charge of electricity that flows between clouds or travels from cloud to ground and ground to cloud—in a split second!

A lightning bolt heats the air to 54,000 degrees Fahrenheit. This intense heat causes the air to expand at the speed of sound, and that creates the noise we hear as thunder. If the storm is right overhead, the thunder sounds like a big bang. But if the storm is farther away, we hear the thunder rumbling for several seconds.

What causes a thundercloud?

Another name for a thundercloud is *cumulonimbus* (KYOOM yuh luh NIM bus). *Cumulous* is a fluffy, puffy-looking cloud. *Nimbus* is a dark rain or snow cloud. The combination of the two means a storm cloud or thundercloud.

How big do thunderclouds get?

A thundercloud may be several miles wide and over 35,000 feet high.

A cumulonimbus cloud is a storm cloud.

What goes on inside a thundercloud?

Think about the way bar magnets work. We know that opposites attract. If you try to join two positives, they will repel each other. But if you bring a positive and a negative close, they will attract one another.

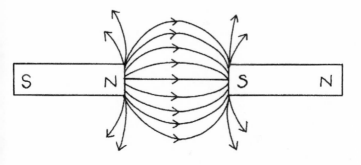

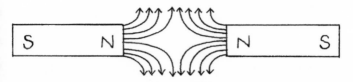

There are positive and negative particles of matter in a thundercloud. These particles are called *protons* and *electrons*. Both kinds have electrical charges. Protons carry a positive charge. Electrons have a negative charge. So protons and electrons are opposites that attract.

The picture shows electrons with negative and positive charges.

The positive-charged protons in a storm cloud are light. So they rise to the top of the cloud. The negative electrons are heavier. They tend to stay near the bottom of the cloud. The rising and falling of air within a cloud separates the positive and negative charges and also bounces them together. Lightning results from the buildup and discharge of electrical energy between the positively and negatively charged areas.

How big is a lightning bolt?

A lightning bolt is three to four miles long. It's about an inch in diameter. Yet it's five times hotter than the sun!

What makes lightning look like it has branches?

Negative charged electrons zigzag down from a cloud in branch-like steps. Each step is about 150 feet long. Each series of steps is called a *stepped leader*. A positive charge from the ground rises to meet the stepped leader. This is called the *return stroke*.

How fast does the return stroke travel?

The return stroke travels upward at 60,000 miles per second! Stepped leaders and return strokes occur two or three or even more times in a row. The steps happen so fast that you can't see them with the naked eye. You can only see the bright flash. That bright flash is what we call lightning.

Do all lightning strikes look the same?

No. To most people, a lightning bolt looks like a zigzagging streak or a flash of bright light like the stepped leader. However, scientists say that there are other types of lightning. These other types of lightning are rare.

There is *ball lightning* that occurs after a ground flash. The ball can be the size of a grapefruit or as large as a watermelon! There is *cloud lightning*—lightning that stays among the clouds and never reaches the ground. Then there is *spider lightning*. Spider lightning can crawl along the sky for up to ninety miles!

ball lightning

cloud lightning

spider lightning

Where does lightning occur?

Do you live in a moist, warm climate? Then you probably have more lightning storms than people who live in other parts of the country. Florida is the lightning capital of the nation. Areas between Tampa and Orlando are hit the most. Do you live in the northwest? States in the northwest are hit the least.

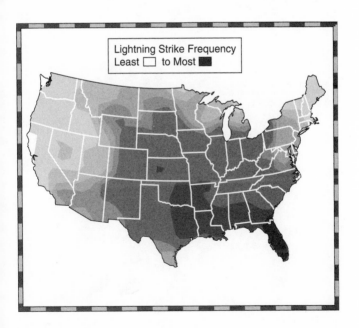

In the United States, most lightning storms occur in July. Lightning can travel sixty miles or more. That's why it's difficult to pinpoint exactly where it will strike.

Which comes first—lightning or thunder?

Lightning comes first. In fact, it's lightning that causes thunder. When lightning occurs, a great deal of heated air is created. The heated air expands and vibrates, and causes the trembling sounds we call *thunder*. So lightning and thunder go hand in hand.

Why do we see lightning before we hear thunder?

Lightning travels fast—*very* fast. That's because light travels 186,000 miles a second. Sound, on the other hand, travels about $\frac{1}{5}$ mile a second. If you see a flash of lightning, count the seconds to the time of the thunder. Divide that number by five to calculate the distance to the storm.

Let's say you counted fifteen seconds. Fifteen divided by five equals three. This means that the lightning is three miles away. What if you see lightning but don't hear any thunder? That means the storm is probably more than fifteen miles away.

When does lightning occur?

Lightning occurs mostly during rainstorms. However, you may see lightning during a snowstorm, a sandstorm, a hurricane, a tornado, or even a volcanic explosion.

What is Saint Elmo's fire?

Many sailors, mountain climbers, and airline pilots have seen a spooky glow called *Saint Elmo's fire*. When misty air surrounds an airplane wing or tip of a sailing mast, electrons from the air are pulled toward the positive charge of the object. This makes the air glow green. Saint Elmo's fire may look weird, but it is harmless. It doesn't damage the objects it touches.

Some say that Saint Elmo's fire is the reason for Ferdinand Magellan's successful trip around the world in 1519. The crew was tired of all the stormy weather they had been having. Suddenly, they saw Saint Elmo's fire on their ships' masts. They took this as a sign from heaven that the ocean would calm. Sure enough, the weather turned calm and they were able to keep sailing!

Is there anything good about lightning?

Lightning changes some of the oxygen in the air into *ozone,* which helps clean the air. That's why everything smells fresh and clean after an electrical storm.

There is another way lightning helps the environment. Our atmosphere contains nitrogen and other chemicals. Plants and animals need nitrogen to live. However, they can't use the nitrogen in its pure form in the atmosphere. Nitrogen has to be joined with other chemicals in order for plants and animals to get its benefit. The energy that lightning produces helps nitrogen combine with other chemicals.

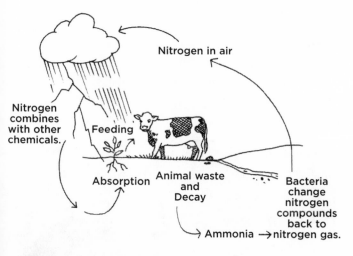

Lightning plays a role in the nitrogen cycle.

Does lightning have any other benefits?

Yes. For one thing, lightning was the only source of fire for early peoples. Every year, lightning causes forest fires that destroy millions of trees. However, these fires also serve a useful purpose. They get rid of *underbrush*, the bushes and shrubs that grow under large trees. This creates space for new plants and trees to grow.

Today, some scientists have a theory. They think that lightning may have helped create life on Earth. The Earth's early atmosphere contained different substances, such as hydrogen and water vapor. Lightning may have produced the energy to turn these substances into molecules. (Molecules are the smallest parts of a substance.) The first molecules rained down into the world's oceans. Eventually, they grew into early life forms.

Forest fires do not just cause damage. They also help make way for new life.

What else can lightning create?

The heat from lightning is so hot, it can melt sand and form what is called a *fulgarite* (FULL gah right). The melted sand forms a hollow tube. The longest fulgarite is listed in the *Guinness Book of World Records*. It was found in Florida in 1996. That fulgarite had two branches. One measured seventeen feet. The other measured sixteen feet.

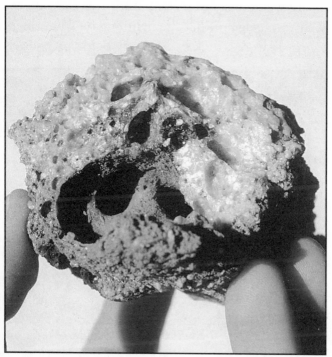

Fulgarite from Arizona

Can lightning be admired as an art form?

A sculptor named Walter de Maria came up with a unique idea. He wanted to combine the science of lightning with art. He set up *The Lightning Field*. *The Lightning Field* consists of four hundred stainless steel lightning rods planted in a grid that is almost a mile square. Walter de Maria put his creation in the desert in southwest New Mexico. That's where many scientists study weather activity. Can you imagine what the lightning rods look like when they are struck by lightning bolts?

Walter de Maria's *The Lightning Field*

3

Beliefs about Lightning

In ancient times, people didn't know what caused lightning. So they made up stories to explain it. Early peoples believed that lightning was "magic fire." The ancient Greeks believed that lightning belonged to the god Zeus, king of all gods. The Greeks thought Zeus used lightning to control humans.

In China, people thought the goddess of lightning traveled with the thunder god. The goddess carried mirrors in her hands. The mirrors would flash a bright light so the thunder god could see where to send his thunderbolts. Later in time, Navajo Indians believed that lightning had healing powers. They pictured lightning as being a thunderbird flapping its huge wings.

Modern beliefs about lightning are quite different from ancient ones. Here are some myths and facts.

Lightning doesn't strike the same place twice.
False. In fact, the Empire State Building in New York City is struck more than twenty times each year! Other towers and tall buildings are also struck many times.

You should never touch a person who has been struck by lightning.
False. A person struck by lightning doesn't carry any electrical charge. In fact, that person may be in need of immediate care. A lightning strike victim may stop breathing and need CPR. If you see someone get struck, call 911 immediately.

Lightning never strikes water.
False. Lightning can strike a body of water, or water that is on land or high in the mountains.

If you are wearing rubber-soled shoes, you'll be safe.
False. Electricity can travel right through rubber, so your shoes will not keep you safe.

A car is a safe place to be during a lightning storm.
True. The metal of a car is somewhat like a lightning rod. The electrical charge travels along the metal parts of the car. But the rubber tires *ground* the car. That means that if lightning strikes

the car, it will travel through the metal and into the ground without hurting you. Be sure not to touch any metal inside the car, such as a radio dial or door handle!

Once lightning has hit the ground, you are safe. False. When lightning hits the ground, it spreads out along the surface of the ground in increasing circles of energy called *ground current*. If lightning contacts a fence or a water pipe or wire entering a house, it can travel quite a distance and injure people near these paths. *Never lie flat on the ground.* Instead, crouch down to make yourself as small as possible.

4

Tales of Survival— and Tips

The odds of being struck by lightning are one in six hundred thousand! So, don't sweat it. Nevertheless, about fifteen hundred people a year are struck by lightning in the United States. Of these, between one hundred fifty and three hundred are killed.

People who have been struck by lightning have reported hearing a short, high-pitched whine. Then they smelled sulfur or something burning. Many people don't remember a thing. They wake up dazed and may find that they have been thrown several feet. Some people have had their clothes blown right off them!

Tales

For the record, Roy C. Sullivan may be one of the luckiest people on Earth. Roy was struck by lightning a total of seven times! And he survived them all!

You would probably agree that Kevin Parent is lucky to be alive. Kevin was struck by lightning three different times. What has Kevin learned from his experiences? Kevin says that he doesn't walk in the rain anymore!

In Oslo, Norway, a lightning bolt hit a house and traveled through the electric wiring. It struck a couple's cast-iron bed and lit up their bedroom. They weren't hurt. But still, they spent the rest of the night on the sofa!

Tips

The safest place to be during a storm is indoors. Stay away from doors, windows, and electrical appliances. Don't use the telephone. Don't take a bath. Just wait out the storm.

If you are outdoors, don't carry an umbrella. The metal rod could attract lightning. Don't go inside a tent. A tent pole can attract lightning. Stay away from any metal objects, such as bikes or metal fences. Don't stand under a tree or on high ground. Lightning usually hits tall objects or metal objects. So just make sure that *you're* not the tallest target in the area!

Conclusion

Some scientists use rockets to trigger lightning in thunderclouds. When the rocket is struck, it acts as a lightning rod, down which lightning can travel. From a safe shelter on the ground, scientists study this human-made lightning.

Other scientists are using lasers to guide and control lightning. The scientists want to know how to keep lightning away from people and buildings. Sometimes, special airplanes are used to study and measure thunderclouds.

Someday, scientists will know even more about lightning. In the meantime, we can all enjoy lightning's splendor—from a safe distance!

A Boeing 737 during a flight test in a storm